Book 4

A Logical Approach to Spelling

Highly Structured Curriculum based on the sound
in words and the application of spelling rules.

Jurina Dean

The Journey

I can still picture the towering pile of research—about a meter high—that I gathered to teach my little girl. It felt like I had no choice but to transform all that precious information into a book. Honestly, I never imagined I'd become the author of these spelling books! Sometimes, what we take on feels much bigger than our own capabilities. But with hard work, endurance, patience, and the right guidance, these books are now out in the world. A heartfelt thank you to all my family and friends who supported me on this journey. I truly appreciate each of you. A very special thank you to Hannah, my sister-in-law. Without you, this book would not have been such a great success! Our greatest joy comes from knowing so many will benefit from this book!

Index

1. Preface
2. Reading & spelling book 4
3. What a typical week with this book looks like
4. Ow! That hurts! Written "ow" and "ou"
5. O so good! More ways to write the name of "o"
6. "o" sound written with "aw" "au" "al" "ough(t)" and "augh(t)"
7. A closer look at "ic" "ure" "ue" "ew"
8. "age", "ui" and the Greek "y"
9. "c" and "g" being a loud sound!
10. "i" before "e" …..
11. Prefixes
12. The "ch" being soft and loud.
13. Words ending in "ive" and "ain"
14. Now this is challenging…."ar" "er" "ir" "or" "ur" "erve" and "our"
15. The "shuhn" sound written "sion" "tion" "cion" "cian"
16. Words ending in "tial" "cial" "cient" tious" "cious"
17. The sound "uhl" and the many ways to write it "il" "el" "al" "le"
18. Was that "ible" or "able"? What about "ibility" or "ability"?
19. Let us look at "ance" "ancy" "ence" "ency"
20. A Closer look at "ery" "ory" & "ary"
21. Numbers Days Months Seasons & Abbreviations
22. Mnemonics
23. The challenge is on!
24. That "e" & "o" sound in words like pleasure, beware, hair, store, floor, pour…….can cause so much trouble if digested at the wrong time.
25. Answers to exercises

Preface

Welcome to the journey of helping your child learn to read and write in English! I invite you to pause and take a moment to explore this preface, as it sets the stage for the incredible impact this book can have on your child's learning experience.

As a mother of four living in Geneva, Switzerland, I understand the unique challenges and opportunities that come with raising children in a multi language environment. My eldest daughter breezed through her weekly spelling lists, effortlessly mastering each word. However, my second daughter faced a different path. The frustration she experienced with her spelling lists was palpable. While she could learn words, recalling them a week later felt like an insurmountable task.

After discovering that she had dyslexia and short-term verbal memory challenges, I embarked on a five-year journey of learning and discovering how to work through the curriculum using an alternative method.

I was advised to focus on the 300 most frequently used words in English. We dedicated a year to mastering these words, achieving a 50% success rate. While this was a start, I knew there had to be a better way. My daughter excelled in math, successfully following logical steps to solve problems. This inspired me to research a logical approach to spelling.

In my quest to find effective resources, I explored many different books and countless online materials. I realised that a vast amount of these resources lacked the structure and repetition necessary for lasting retention.

While I couldn't find a single definitive resource, I began piecing together a beautiful method for learning to spell in English—one that emphasises a logical structure, much like maths. This book aims to provide that framework.

In English spelling, we often encounter exceptions to the rule, but we'll tackle these later in our journey. Initially, we focus on what makes sense phonetically and explore homophones as a key theme throughout this book. Together, we'll play detective, investigating the fascinating world of different spellings. As a child's brain develops, they will naturally anchor these "exception to the rule" words.

Our curriculum provides a strong foundation and support for visual memory and logical thinking. We cover all spelling elements of national curriculums, but with a difference — we emphasise the sounds in words and foster confidence in blending simple words for future success.

We'll explore "borrowed" words from other languages, highlighting the similarities that can serve as helpful anchors. Towards the end of the series, we'll address words that often cause confusion early on for children who find spelling challenging. These words will align correctly in your child's mind as they mature, so we won't focus on teaching them prematurely. Instead, we'll nurture their spelling confidence in stages of mind-readiness.

At the end of each section, you'll find a word bank. Use this to create spelling tests until your child masters each word, revisiting it throughout the series. Be mindful of your child's attention span, and keep lessons between 10 to 30 minutes a day. Consistent, short repetitions are key! Help them understand why words are spelled a certain way, and revisit the word bank after a month, and again after three months.

You are making a wonderful difference to your child's learning journey! Enjoy every moment of this experience—it truly passes quickly. Happy learning together!

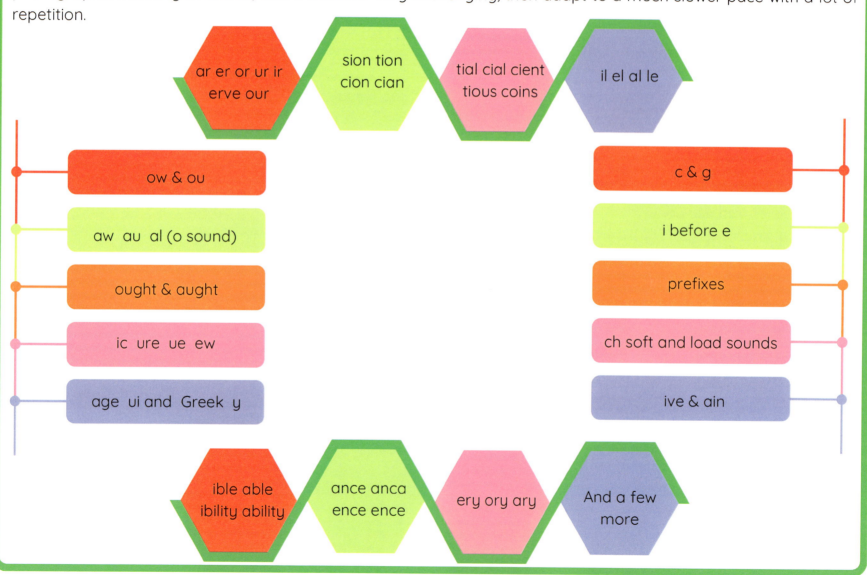

What a typical week with this book looks like

Daily practice of reading, writing, and spelling is essential, and it should be fun! Pay attention to your child's focus and adjust the pace as needed. Think of their attention span as a muscle that we are gradually strengthening. We can create a consistent structure for lessons or mix things up, based on your child's energy on the day. On some days, starting with a spelling test followed by new activities can work well.

Make sure to celebrate each achievement, no matter how small! Remember, the key is to review concepts regularly and keep the learning experience joyful.

To summarise

- Learning a concept once a week, reviewing it daily.
- Spelling test 30-40 words twice a week.
- Exercises
- Reading 30 mins a day

Ow! That hurts!   Written ow & ou

ow

The <u>brown</u> <u>owl</u> sits on the <u>towel</u> in a <u>tower</u>.

Learn this!!

- ...and any words that are similar to these
- ow sound followed by

-n -l -er or -el

frow**n**
tow**n**
dow**n**
clow**n**
drow**n**
tow**er**
flow**er**
pow**er**
vow**el**
cow
row *

Homophone
flour vs flower
Remember the flower with the "w", is for flowers that grow long and short.
To make a "w" you go up and down - long and short

ou

cloud
loud
shout
proud
bound
found
pound
round
sound
ground
hound

hous**e**
mous**e**
spous**e**

sour *
our
hour
flour

mouth
south
count
trout
out
lounge

hound

Learn these!
- A house is not without people. ➡ add "e"
- A mouse is in the house. ➡ both get "e"
- A spouse needs another spouse. ➡ add "e"

These words are quite tricky.
At what **hour** will you be at **our** house?
Remember in French we don't always pronounce the "h" at the beginning of a word. French hour....

There are more rules we can add here, but it does complicate matters and we need to keep it as simple as possible.

Ow! That hurts! Written ow & ou

OW   The br**ow**n **owl** sits on a
tow**el** in the tow**er**.

fr**ow**n
t**ow**n
d**ow**n
cl**ow**n
dr**ow**n
tow**er**
flow**er**
pow**er**
vow**el**
c**ow**
r**ow** *

OU   She is so pr**ou**d to have f**ou**nd a p**ou**nd on the
gr**ou**nd. He sh**ou**ts l**ou**d from on top of the cl**ou**d.

cloud loud shout proud bound found
hound pound round sound ground

The mouse is alone in the house with his spouse.

The tr**ou**t sh**ou**ts with its m**ou**th.

In an h**ou**r, he will be s**ou**r because
he drank **ou**r lemon juice.

flour vs **flower**

Take your time repeating these words. We add another "ow" spelling that is not a sharp
sound. So really get familiar with these "ow" and "ou" words before you move on.

Fill in ou or ow and check your answers

fr _ _ n 😠   sp _ _ se
h _ _ r   br _ _ n
cl _ _ d   fl _ _ er
t _ _ n   r _ _ nd
m _ _ se   p _ _ er
s _ _ r   tr _ _ t
d _ _ n   m _ _ th
cl _ _ n   v _ _ el
dr _ _ n   fl _ _ r
_ _ r   t _ _ er

Sound {O} (the o says its name - "o" in program) - written ow

A little bit of revision and then the new addition ow for {O}

Sound "o" says its name {O} ("o" in programme) (not "o" for orange)

When two vowels go walking, the first one does the talking ...it says its name

- o + e   oe {O}
- o + a   oa {O}
- o _ e   {O} "e" at the end of the word, makes the vowel says its name
- pr**o**gramme   "o" in open syllable   {O}

t**oe**	nos**e**	hormone
foe	bone	alone
potatoes	sole	envelope
tomatoes	cone	(remember
heroes	hope	envelope has 3
	drone	sides = 3 "e"s in
g**oa**t	home	the word)
boat	note	
coat	globe	
road	tone	programme
oak	phone	proclaim
oats	rope	motion
soap	joke	
loaf		
toad		

ow

shallow
mellow
yellow
fellow
pillow
follow
hollow
arrow
narrow
borrow
sorrow
throw
tow
mow
rainbow
slowly
shadow
elbow

Most of the time, there is no consonant after the ow sound. You hear the ow sound last.

Homophone
b**o**rrow
borough
b**u**rrow

Rabbits live in **burrow**s.
city district = **borough**
Can I **borrow** your pen? Will you lend it to me?

I can lend you my pencil, and you can borrow my pencil.

Sound {O} (the o says its name - "o" in program) - written ow

Homophones

borrow

You can borrow books from the library.

burrow

The rabbits made a burrow at the end of the garden.

borough

A high proportion of young people live in that borough.

groan

Every morning when the old man goes for a walk, he groans.

grown

The son is looking after his grandmother who has grown very old now.

The tree has grown very fast this spring.

Complete the sentences with the wordbook below

home   grown   borough   burrow   slowly   toad
borrow   shallow   narrow   follow   hope

The path is not wide. It is _____narrow_____
Will you lend me your pen? Can I _____borrow_____ it?
The city council looks after one _____borough_____ (area).
The rabbit lives in a _____burrow_____
One should not give up. But have _____hope_____
He is driving too fast. He should drive more _____slowly_____
It is not a frog but it looks similar. It is called a t_____oad_____
The river is deep, not _____shallow_____
He has _____grown_____ so much taller.
Copy me. Do as I do. F_____ollow_____ me.
After school we are going _____home_____

Answers are in the back of the book

Write a word for each picture. They all have an {O} sound in them - "o" saying its name.

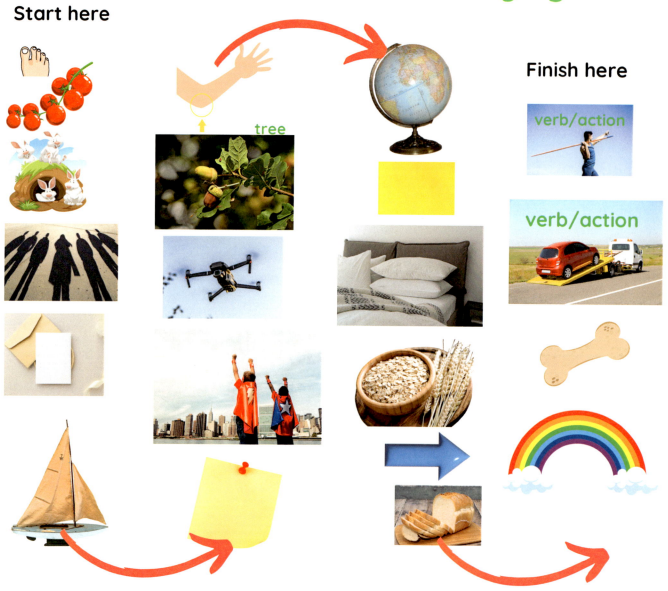

Words

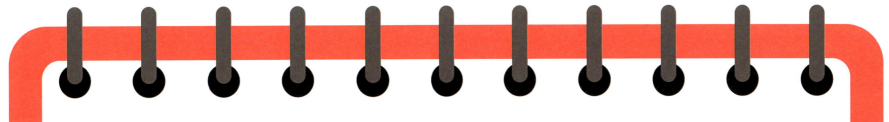

Answers in the back of the book

Circle the correct spelling

The broun/brown owl/oul flew through the clowd/cloud doun/down to the grownd/ground.

He saw a big, broun/brown, fat mouse/mows. He shouted/showted at the mows/mouse. Then he flew with all his pour/power up to the tour/tower.

The man came out/owt of the hows/house and frouned/frowned at the couw/cow.

Everyone looked doun/down to the grownd/ground with a froun/frown making no sound/sownd.

I hope/hoap to follo/follow the rainbow/rainboe. My shadow/shado, sloly/slowly follows/folloes me.

Answers in the back of the book

The sound "o" written aw au al ough(t) and augh(t)

aw
saw	hawk
jaw	coleslaw
straw	squawk
paw	prawn
draw	awful
yawn	flawless
claw	
crawl	

au
author	laundry
autumn	caution
pause	fault
cause	launched
saucer	launch
sauce	haunted
applause	August
applaud	astronaut

Very tricky some of these…a lot of repetition and patience required!

al
- talk
- bald
- chalk
- walk
- wall
- fall
- ball

ough(t)
buy	bought
bring	brought
fight	fought
think	thought
sight	sought

augh(t)
te**a**ch	taught
c**a**tch	caught
	naughty
	slaughter
d**a**d & d**a**ughter	daughter

The sound "o" written aw au al ough(t) and augh(t)

ough(t)   augh(t)

buy	bought	teach	taught
bring	brought	catch	caught
fight	fought		naughty
think	thought		slaughter
seek	sought	dad & daughter	daughter

Hint: Looking at the present tense of these words, you will see that if there is an "a" in the present tense, then there is an "a" in the past tense. If there is no "a" in the present tense form of the word, then there is no "a" in the past tense of the word. The sound is exactly the same but written differently.

Rewrite the words in bold

I **saw** that when he **draws**, he **yawns** with his jaw wide open.

Can a **hawk** pick up a **straw** with his **claw** when it **squawks?**

The cat **crawls** on all four **paws** to catch an **awful prawn.**

---

talk
bald
chalk
walk

Connect the words to the pictures

Look at these words and notice the different ways to spell the same sound "o". Connect each word to the the correct picture.

tall   wall

roll   talk

toll   walk

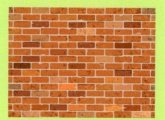

chalk   bald

The sound "o" written as aw au al ough(t) and augh(t)

Choose one word in bold for each picture and write the underneath the picture.

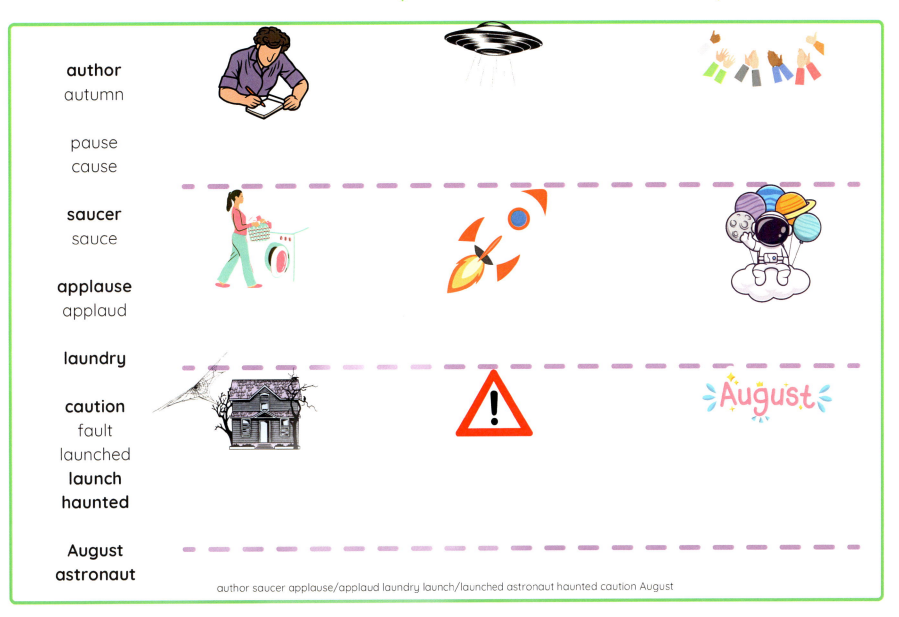

The spelling of ough, ought & aught creates different sounds

buy	bought
bring	brought
fight	fought
think	thought
seek	sought
te**a**ch	t**a**ught
c**a**tch	c**a**ught

There is no "a" in present tense!

Everytime you spell these words, remind yourself to write the present tense first……

Number **0** zero is referred to as n**o**ught sometimes.

That boy is n**a**ughty not nice.

Repeat this group of words together and often.

bought   brought
thought   taught

**through   though   tough
thorough   thought   throw**

rough   tough   enough
plough   dough   though

He was taught how to do it.
He thought of what he did on the weekend..
The test was tough even though he studied through the holidays.

The spelling of ough, ought & aught creates different sounds

**through   though   tough
thorough thought throw**

**rough tough enough
plough dough though**

He was <u>taught</u> how to do it.
He <u>thought</u> of what he did on the weekend..
The test was <u>tough</u> even <u>though</u> he studied <u>through</u> the holidays.

The spelling of ough, ought & aught creates different sounds

Connect the picture with the matching word, and write the word in the correct sentence.
Some of the words don't have a matching picture.

bought
brought

I _____ many things at the shop.
My sister _____ me dinner.

thought
taught
through
though
tough

It was a _____ match yesterday.
The grass is long, even _____ we cut it yesterday.
He _____ about it before he did it.
The teacher _____ us a lesson.
The car burst _____ the wall.

rough
enough
plough
dough

She prepares the _____ to make bread.
The farmers _____ the field.
No more cold drinks. You have had _____
No more noise. That is e _____
He had a _____ day at work.
The surface is not smooth. It is _____

Answers in the back of the book.

A few more sounds and the way we write them

1 syllable words → write them with "**ick**"
(brick sick kick)

2+ syllable words → write them with "**ic**"

ic

panic	Arctic	Atlantic	cosmetic
tropic	attic	gigantic	traffic
athletic	metric	picnic	public
tragic	classic	antiseptic	magic
domestic	fantastic	chaotic	lunatic
horrific	logic	automatic	basic
plastic	comic	romantic	elastic
			energetic
			music
			electric
			majestic
			mechanic

Refer to these as "ic words"

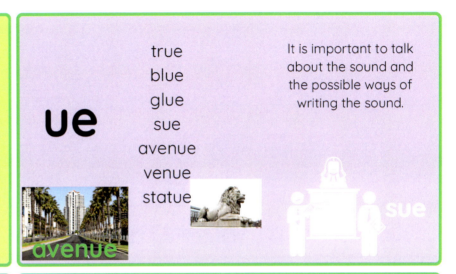

ue

true
blue
glue
sue
avenue
venue
statue

It is important to talk about the sound and the possible ways of writing the sound.

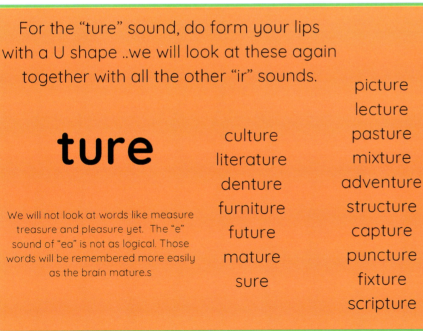

For the "ture" sound, do form your lips with a U shape ..we will look at these again together with all the other "ir" sounds.

ture

culture
literature
denture
furniture
future
mature
sure

picture
lecture
pasture
mixture
adventure
structure
capture
puncture
fixture
scripture

We will not look at words like measure treasure and pleasure yet. The "e" sound of "ea" is not as logical. Those words will be remembered more easily as the brain mature.s

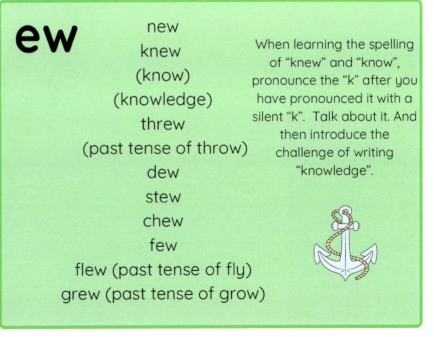

ew

new
knew
(know)
(knowledge)
threw
(past tense of throw)
dew
stew
chew
few
flew (past tense of fly)
grew (past tense of grow)

When learning the spelling of "knew" and "know", pronounce the "k" after you have pronounced it with a silent "k". Talk about it. And then introduce the challenge of writing "knowledge".

Rewrite these sentences with the correct spelling.

1. The blu statu was captered in a pictur. (4)
2. We panick every time she drives down the avenu to the venu. (3)
3. It is always an adventur tracking down crawling creaturs. (2)
4. The energetick boy likes riding his bicycle. (1)
5. I no a tric that he already new. (3)
6. I thro the ball to him. He can catch a feu balls. (2)
7. I like eating green peace. (1)
8. The world will be a better place if there is more piece. (1)
9. I always give my friend a bigger peas of cake. (1)
10. He is very polite. He always says pease. (1)

Answers in the back of the book.

Sentences with the correct spelling.

Word bank

saw	laundry						majestic
jaw	caution						mechanic
straw	fault		brown	cloud	toe	panic	chaotic
paw	launched		owl	loud	foe	tropic	automatic
draw	launch		tower	shout	potatoes	athletic	romantic
yawn	haunted		towel	proud	hereos	tragic	
claw	August			bound	alone	domestic	picture
crawl	astronaut		frown	found	envelope	horrific	lecture
hawk			town	hound	drone	plastic	pasture
coleslaw	bought	Remember to	down	pound	goat	Atlantic	mixture
squawk	brought	prompt the present	clown	round	road	gigantic	adventure
prawn	fought	tense if getting	drown	sound	toad	Arctic	structure
awful	thought ←	stuck with spelling	tower	ground		attic	capture
flawless	sought	of these words.	flower		shallow	metric	puncture
			power	mouth	mellow	classic	fixture
talk	taught ←		vowel	south	yellow	fantastic	scripture
bald	caught		cow	count	fellow	logic	culture
chalk	naughty		row	trout	pillow	comic	literature
walk	n**o**ught			out	grown	picnic	denture
wall	slaughter					antiseptic	furniture
fall	daughter		flower		follow	cosmetic	future
ball			flour	hous**e**	hollow	traffic	mature
	thought			mouse	arrow	public	sure
author	through		flew	spouse	narrow	magic	
autumn	tough		knew		borrow	lunatic	true
pause	thorough		(know)	sour	sorrow	basic	blue
cause	though		stew	our	throw	elastic	glue
saucer			chew	h**our**	tow	energetic	avenue
sauce		HAVE	threw	flour	mow	music	venue
applause		FUN	(throw)		rainbow	electric	statue
applaud			dew		slowly		
			few		shadow		
Always put words in context.. Use the same sentence every time you refer to that word.			sew		elbow	borrow borough burrow	

"c" and "g" - loud and soft sound - Revision.

c + a	LOUD c		g + a	LOUD g	
c + o	LOUD c	cat cot cut	g + o	LOUD g	gas got gut
c + u	LOUD c		g + u	LOUD g	

This concept is explained in detail in Book 3!

c + e	SOFT s		g + e	SOFT j	
c + i	SOFT s	cell circle cycle	g + i	SOFT j	gesture giant gym
c + y	SOFT s		g + y	SOFT j	

LOUD c and g ?

gess   g**u**ess   "u" to the rescue!

u comes to the rescue

circit .....circ**u**it.... "u" to the rescue!! OR "k" to the rescue ~~cit~~ **k**it

and "k" at the beginning of a "c" word.

---

c and g loud	+ a o u
c and g soft	+ e i y

c (loud) + e /i/y   kicking "k" to the rescue
eg **k**it

c&g(loud) + e/i/y   "u" to the rescue
eg g**u**ess circ**u**it

SOFT sound (followed by e i y)

g**y**m
g**i**ant
g**e**sture
g**e**l
larg**e**
orang**e**

rec**e**ive
c**y**cle
fenc**e**

With the help of "**u**", "c" & "g" becomes a **LOUD** "k" & "g" sound

g**u**ess
g**u**erilla
bag**u**ette
g**u**ard
dialog**u**e
circ**u**it

Exceptions ....
get girl

-age & Greek y

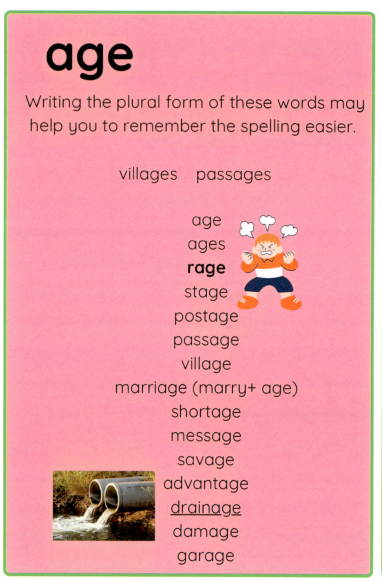

age

Writing the plural form of these words may help you to remember the spelling easier.

villages   passages

age
ages
rage
stage
postage
passage
village
marriage (marry+ age)
shortage
message
savage
advantage
<u>drainage</u>
damage
garage

the greek "i" using the "y"

gym
Egypt
type
pyramids
mystery
myth
crystal
pyjamas
oxygen
typical
syrup

analyse
sympathy
hyphen
synonym
syllable
hymn

-age

Why do we have an "e" after the "g"?

If we want the "g" to be a soft sound it has to be written together with an "e", "i" or "y".

Passage in a book.
Nasal passage.
Passage under the bridge.

age

ages   passage   savage

rage   village   advantage

marriage   drainage

stage   (marry + age)   damage

shortage   garage

postage 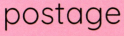   message 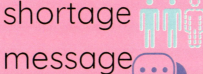   

ui

The spelling "ui" makes the sound "oo" or almost {U}
(Like in "u" for united - 2 vowels go walking, the first one does the talking).

fruit
grapefruit
suit
suitcase
lawsuit
pursuit
recruit
juice
cruise
bruise

However, remember our rule for "c" or "g" followed by "i" "e" or "y"?
These are pronounced with a soft sound!
How do we get the "c" and "g" to be a loud sound when followed by "i" "e" or "y"?

"u" comes to the rescue!   bisc**u**it

biscuit
circuit
guide
disguise

guilt
guilty as charged

guilt
guilty as charged

Complete the words

ui	ui
s _ _ tcase	circ _ _ t
j _ _ ce	s _ _ t
cr _ _ se	purs _ _ t
br _ _ se	recr _ _ t
grapefr _ _ t	bisc _ _ t
age	**age**
post _ _ _	vill _ _ _
mess _ _ _	advant _ _ _
gar _ _ _	sav _ _ _

y	y
g _ m	ox _ gen
s _ llable	t _ pical
p _ ramids	s _ rup
cr _ stals	m _ th
h _ phen	c _ cle
t _ pe	s _ mpathy
s _ non _ _ m	h _ m**n**
m _ stery	p _ jamas
Eg _ pt	anal _ se

i {I} before e {E} except after c {C}

grief
believe
belief
mischief
priest

field
yield
chief
thief
shield
achieve
niece
piece
relief

Homophones
belie**v**e
(is a **v**erb)
belie**f**
(is a noun – your **f**aith)

piece
peas
peace

received
receipt*
perceive
deceive
deceit
conceive
ceiling

Recei**p**t has a "p" in it because we need to **p**ay to get a recei**p**t

There are some exceptions words that have a different story to them.
weird caffeine protein sheik either neither seize

Sh**ei**la & K**ei**th …..see how many you can remember…..

(S**ei**ze the moment! N**ei**ther the sheik nor Sh**ei**la drink caffeine or eat prot**ei**n. Very w**ei**rd.

Put the words in the right column

- believe
- belief
- conceive
- ceiling
- piece
- niece
- perceive
- deceit
- receipt
- shield
- grief
- yield
- received

ie	ei

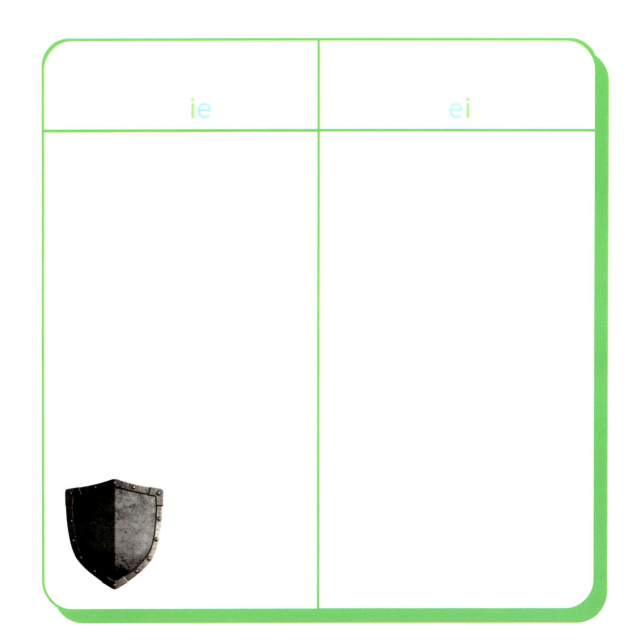

Prefixes

unwell
undressed
unfair
unequal

illegal
illogical
illegible

irregular
irresponsible

impolite
imperfect
immature
impossible

inedible
inhuman
inactive
incapable
incorrect
incurable
invisible
indecisive

Words beginning with **l** ➡ il

Words beginning with **r** ➡ ir

Words beginning with **m** or **p** ➡ im

dislike
disagree
disappear
dishonest
disrespect

misbehave

superfine
supersonic

anticlockwise
antibiotic
antibody
antisocial

foreseen
forehand
forewarn
foreshadow
forecast

extraordinary
extracurricular
exceed
exclusive

defrost
decide

Prefixes
il ir im in anti dis un mis de

Write the word on the left, with a prefix in the box on the right.

appear	When something went missing.
capable	When someone is not capable of do something.
responsible	It was a ….. thing to do.
possible	The task looked ….. Not possible.
decisive	He can`t make a decision. He is …..
behave	They were not listening to their parents. They ………..
understand	They always ……. us when we explain it to them.
frost	I took the frozen meat out of the freezer this morning. Now it is …
equal	They do not have the same amount of sweets. They have an ….. amount.
correct	The answer is not correct.
legal	It is not allowed to chew chewing gum in Singapore. It is ……
regular	His visits to his grandmother is not regular.
polite	That is not a very polite thing to say.
social	It is very ……. to interrupt someone when they are talking.
mature	He is not behaving very mature.
edible	That cake doesn`t look edible.
respect	He doesn`t treat his teacher with respect.
sane	The idea of swimming the English Channel doesn`t sound very sane.
logical	It is not logical thinking to wear a wool jumper when it is sweltering hot.
active	The volcano hasn`t been active for 5 years. It is ………..

The letters "ch" can make different sounds

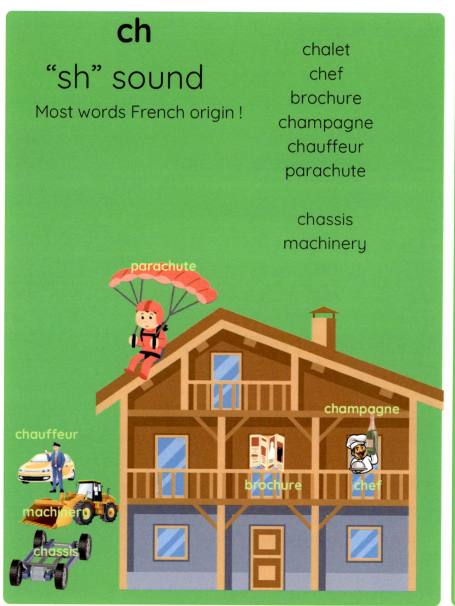

ch
"sh" sound
Most words French origin!

chalet
chef
brochure
champagne
chauffeur
parachute

chassis
machinery

ch
"k" sound
Most words Greek origin!

Chris
mechanic
orchestra
chemistry
choir
technology
schedule
school
echo
character
scheme

Chris has a scheme in school to build a character. He will study chemistry and technology and become a mechanic. He will also be part of the orchestra and sing in the choir till it echoes.

stomach ache
chronic

orchid
monarchy
anchor

**The word choir comes from the Latin word chorus.

orchids

English words that come from Greek origin - the "ch" is pronounced with loud "k" sound.

orchard

Old English for the word orchard is orceard meaning fruit garden. The plum trees in the orchard are coming into blossom soon.

champagne

campaign

together with "-ain" words

The word comes from the French word campagne which means "open country" or "field" and over time became part of English political vocabulary.

By pausing on these words individually, you build anchors that will make them so much easier to remember!

Words ending in "ive" and "ain"

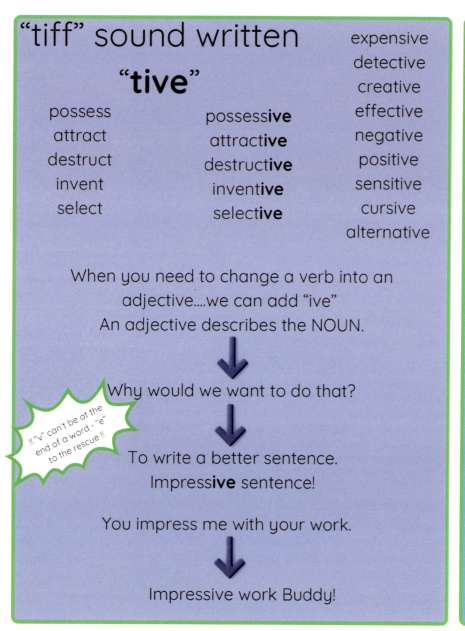

Word bank

age	fruit	field	chalet	
ages	grapefruit	yield	machinery	
rage	suit	chief	chef	homophones
stage	suitcase	thief	brochure	scent and sent
postage	lawsuit	shield	schedule	seen and scene
passage	pursuit	achieve	champagne	
village	recruit	niece	chauffeur	
marriage	juice	piece	chassis	expensive
(marry+	cruise	relief	parachute	detective
age)	bruise	grief		creative
shortage		believe		effective
message	biscuit	belief	anchor	negative
savage	circuit	mischief	mechanic	positive
advantage		priest	chemistry	sensitive
drainage			stomach	cursive
	guide		ache	alternative
	disguise		orchid	
			orchestra	
	gym	Homophones	technology	train
	Egypt	belie**v**e	schedule	refrain
	analyse	(is a **v**erb)	Chris	certain
	hyphen	belie**f**	monarchy	captain
	synonym	(is a noun	choir	fountain
	type	**f**aith)	scheme	bargain
	mystery		chronic	curtain
	myth	piece	school	campain
	syllable	peas	echo	remain
	sympathy	piece	character	mountain
	hymn			detain
	pyjamas			campaign

Correct the spelling mistakes
"ch" "ain" and "ive"

The broshure of the shalet in the mountens looked beautiful.
The sauffeur gave me a glass of shampan on our drive to the shalet.
The sheff prepared a meal while we were busy parasute jumping.
I hope that we can fit it all into our shedule.
He was very positiv about the expensiv detectif work that was done.
They used the latest tecknology mixed with cemistree and got great results.
The scool coir and the orcestra perform at the same time.
The brayn can be trayned to be more positiv.
You are the capten of your ship.
Refrayn from drinking from the founten - the water is not clean.

Answers in the back of the book.

Rewrite the sentences with the correct spelling of the words.

"ir" sound written with
ar er or ir ur ure ier and our

car	vinegar	sort	starter	burn
scar	pillar	shorts	mister	hurt
star	dollar	horse	sister	nurse
scarf	familiar	sport	monster	purse
smart	mustard	fork	enter	church
start	beggar	snort	layer	return
part	scholar	doctor	choker	
hard	popular	donor	prosper	twirl
sharp	singular	scissors	paper	girl
	grammar			shirt
snarl	particular	impostor	version	
sparse	burglar	juror	immersion	thirst
starve	cellar	bachelor		third
embark	muscular	minor		first
harvest	custard	governor		
bargain				
	liar & peculiar			

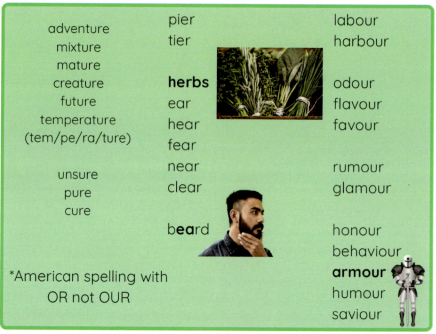

adventure   pier   labour
mixture   tier   harbour
mature
creature   **herbs**
future   ear   odour
temperature hear   flavour
(tem/pe/ra/ture)   favour
             fear
             near   rumour
unsure   clear   glamour
pure
cure
             b**ea**rd   honour
                         behaviour
                         armour
*American spelling with humour
OR not OUR   saviour

are
care
dare
here
there   Homophones
hire
dire   nerve
core   serve   surf   verse
                                           serve
                                           curve
                                           surf

For some learners this part could be challenging. Take it slow. Eventually it will be easy too.

"ir" sound written with
ar er or ir ur ure ier and our

The **burn** on my thumb really **hurts**. The **nurse** treated it. I paid her with money out of my **purse** and then **return**ed to **church**.

burn
hurt
nurse
purse
church
return

The wolf **snarled** at me. He must be starving or **thirsty**.

She came **first** and my sister came t**hird**.

thirst
third
first

The doctor cut particular layers with the **scissors**.

The girl who was wearing a **choker** had a **monster** picture on her shirt. She **immersed** herself in her work.

The fisherman **laboured** at the **harbour** where there was a bad **odour**.

The **horse sort** of **snorted** before he appeared in the gate.

The **beggar**'s circumstances were **dire** before he became a **popular bachelor sports star**.

He looks better   than   the waves.

serve vs surf

Our **saviour** wears his silver **armour** with **honour**.

"ir" sound written with ar er or ir ur ure ier and our

Homophones

hair

hare

The hare is playing catch with the girl who has lots of **hair**.

Here comes the boy who **hears** with his **ears**.

I **dare** you to swim with **sharks**!

The **future favourite flavour** will be **custard**, eaten together with **mustard** and **herbs**.

Write the words with the "ir" sound - ar er or ir ur and our

st _ _ t	mixt _ _ e	b _ _ gain	vineg _ _
sc _ _	s _ _ ve	lab _ _ _	muscul _ _
sp _ _ t	n _ _ ve	glam _ _ _	burgl _ _
b _ _ n	ch _ _ ch	sc _ _ f	g _ _ l
thi _ _ st	fut _ _ e	st _ _ ve	h _ _ se
uns _ _ e	bachel _ _	doct _ _	st _ _ ter
famili _ _	impost _ _	h _ _ vest	fe _ _
f _ _ st	n _ _ se	p _ _ se	cle _ _
c _ _ e	li _ _	sh _ _ ts	creat _ _ e
v _ _ sion	hon _ _ _	sciss _ _ s	st _ _

If you use the American spelling then you need to write "or "instead of "our".

Crossword

Across

3. The knight puts on his a..... (shield helmet etc) before he went into battle.

6. They have very sharp teeth and some can eat you. They live in the sea. sh.....

9. You have to be careful around the fire you can b... yourself.

11. A creature that is not real, but little children can be scared of them. monst...

12. We are going on a trip into the jungle It will be a real adven....

13. A person who gives you medicine when you are sick do...

15. He practically lives on the beach. He s... the waves all day.

16. We use these to cut with and it is very sharp. s...

17. Another way to write 1st.

Down

1. A person asking for money or something to eat. He often doesn't have a home. be...

2. A place where boats park when they are not out at sea. There is normally a lighthouse too. h.....

4. You eat food when you are hungry. You drink water when you are th...

5. The colour of your drink is red. What fl.... is it?

7. He loves tennis. He is very good at s...ing.

8. The desert is very hot in the day and can be very cold at night. The tem..... varies a lot.

9. A person who breaks into your house and steals your goods. b...

10. Depending whether you are naughty or nice, we will go to the beach. It depends on your beh.....

14. Another way to write 3rd. thr..

Answers in the back of the book.

Word search

```
c l d d c t p v e r s e b b p
u p q r h h i r e r u t a m o
r y b i a n u g a s t a r v e
v u r u e t d r u h m r g s t
e d a g r e s r c u s a a r b
t m a g s g f u m h r g i o m
h r b r a i l i m a f g n s u
i b a a e r x a l c k e c s s
r p e s r t o u r r v b l i c
s m r a u k p l e r u m r c u
t u g r r o f s e r p o a s l
n e e r p d i n e h u w n v a
p a r t i c u l a r c t s o r
r a i l u c e p k k v a u x h
t s r i f u g p u r s e b f h
```

bachelor	beard	bargain
beggar	church	burglar
curve	familiar	embark
first	honour	future
mature	muscular	mixture
mustard	nurse	nerve
particular	popular	peculiar
purse	serve	scissors
sharp	sparse	snarl
starve	third	surf
thirst	vinegar	verse

Word bank

car	sort	girl	labour	nerve
scar	shorts	shirt	harbour	verse
star	horse			serve
scarf	sport	**thirst**	odour	curve
smart	fork	**third**	flavour	surf
start	snort	**first**	favour	
part	doctor			
hard	donor	adventure		
sharp	scissors	mixture	rumour	
snarl		mature	glamour	
sparse	impostor	creature		
starve	juror	future	honour	
embark	bachelor	temperature	behaviour	
harvest	minor	(tem/pe/ra/ture)	armour	
bargain	governor	unsure	humour	
vinegar	starter	pure	saviour	
pillar	mister	cure		
dollar	sister			
familiar	monster	pier	are	
mustard	enter	tier	care	
beggar	layer	herbs	dare	
scholar	choker	ear	here	
popular	prosper	hear	there	
singular	paper	fear	hire	
grammar	version	near	dire	
particular	immersion	clear	core	
burglar		beard		
cellar	burn			
muscular	hurt			
custard	nurse			
liar	purse			
peculiar	church			
	return			

wallet < purse < handbag

The sound "shuhn" written -sion -tion -cion -cian

-tion

Most of the time we use the ending -tion !!! A lot of the words has a Latin origin.
Looking at the root word will give you an indication of how to write the "shuhn" sound.

information	condition	emotion
addition	station	creation
action	population	addition
motion	invitation	subtraction
direction	combination	perfection
vacation	direction	inspection
mention	opposition	preparation
attention	devotion	relaxation
decoration	pollution	education
correction		

-cian

Most occupation/job descriptions the "shuhn" sound is written with -cian.

electrician
politician
magician
musician
optician
mathematician
b**eau**tician

(look at the French spelling "eau" for water. (It will help you)

-cion

suspicion

From the French word suspicion.

Clue!

root word ends with "t"   + tion

subtrac**t** + ? (tion) = subtraction

root word ends with "s"   +sion

revi**s**e + ? (sion) = revision

root word ends with "te"   drop "e" + tion

popula**te** + ? (tion) = population

-sion

tension	occasion	prosession
permission	convulsion	fashion
possession	confession	omission
revision	submission	explosion
expansion	supervision	cushion
decision	inclusion	impression
permission	emulsion	expression
pension	mansion	succession
mission	propulsion	
invasion	suspension	
vision	admission	

Connect the correct "shuhn" sound ending

tion

sion

electric
combine
revise
explode
suspense
politics
devote
correct
mathematic
educate
decide
supervise
beauty

cian

cion

Answers in the back of the book.

Word search

```
j g i f p l n x n s m v i n p
w k n w n e e a f x i x o t o
e r l t o p n f i n s i m s l
n o i s i v z s a c s r a e l
l n w g s u n i i s i p y i u
d a c b n y c d i o o g n i t
t i s g e i n m p r n v a o i
l c c t t i r o q e a a l m o
n i l p p e r m i s s i o n n
o s o p p b w d i t u r z m x
i u i r v i n o i c i p s u s
t m a l v f n d i m a d s n q
a p o p u l a t i o n d n i f
t h u k w n a i c i t i l o p
s m a t h e m a t i c i a n c
```

magician	invasion	condition
musician	mission	mathematician
permission	pension	optician
pollution	politician	permission
suspicion	station	population
	vision	tension

-tial /-cial, -cious/-tious and -cient endings

tial or cial
Distinguish by practising saying these words with tial "sh" sound formed lower down in your mouth and cial "s" sound formed to the font in your mouth.

special
official
social
especially

torrential
circumstantial
initial
essential
confidential
partial

-cient

ancient
patient
sufficient
efficient

old

not too much
not too little
just enough

multitasking

-cious

precious
spacious
delicious
gracious
suspicious
vicious
conscious

Look at the root words of these....

space
delicacy
grace

health conscious

-tious

ambitious (determine)
cautious (careful)

fictitious (imaginary)
scrumptious

Look at the root words of these....
ambition
caution
fiction

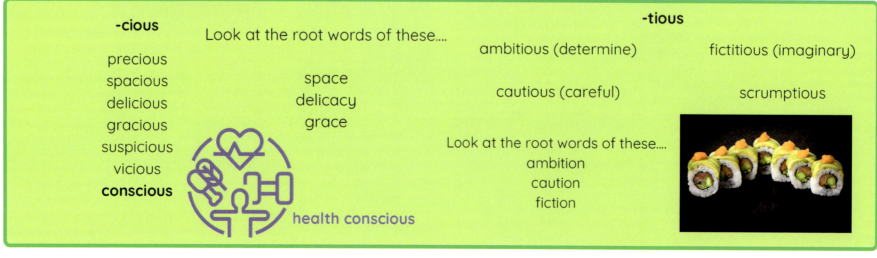

Put the words in the right column

- torren-
- spe-
- circumstan-
- ini-
- espe-(ly)
- so-
- par-
- offi-
- confiden-
- essen-

tial	cial

Answers in the back of the book

Words ending with the sound "uhl". Different spelling il el al ul le

IL EL AL

We do NOT write -le after the following consonants : m n r v w & soft c

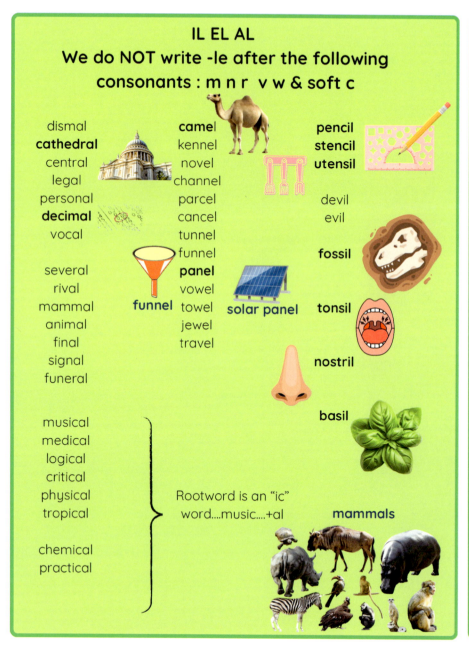

dismal
cathedral
central
legal
personal
decimal
vocal

several
rival
mammal
animal
final
signal
funeral

musical
medical
logical
critical
physical
tropical

chemical
practical

camel
kennel
novel
channel
parcel
cancel
tunnel
funnel
panel
vowel
towel
jewel
travel

pencil
stencil
utensil

devil
evil

fossil

tonsil

nostril

basil

Rootword is an "ic" word....music....+al

mammals

LE

Bible
grumble
cable
table
wobble
scramble
bubble
nibble
scribble
double
trouble
gamble
bobble
tumble

cuticle
cubicle
circle
uncle
article
miracle
cubicle
vehicle
obstacle
icicle
tentacle

example
apple
maple
ample
steeple
cripple
ripple
staple
sample
trample
temple
simple
purple
people

cradle
ladle
poodle
doodle
noodle
puddle
needle
paddle

cuddle
muddle
riddle
candle

rifle
raffle
sniffle
shuffle

brittle
kettle
beetle
battle
cattle
rattle
little
gentle
startle
turtle

jungle
giggle
angle
jiggle
wiggle
eagle
single
juggle
snuggle
struggle

wrestle
castle

tickle
crackle
shackle
tackle
speckle
freckle
pickle
fickle
crinkle
sprinkle
twinkle
wrinkle
buckle

drizzle
muzzle
nozzle
puzzle
frazzle

muzzle

Word search

```
y e k j l m l a e q j e l l o
s c l a e a w l i l u l a i i
f p v g r w p x p o n g r r e
l i e e a p e h a g g e t d
r a v c i e y l c i l u v s r
y e n r k s s u l c e r e o i
s l c i i l b b a a q t s n z
l n i c f i e r r l y s t q z
a a a s c g i f d v j u g t l
n l m l n d e y e l d n a c e
g l e s d e d n h t u n n e l
i r j l i e t b t m a m m a l
s g e q q d m u a l a m i n a
e x a m p l e d c t e q x h n
l a c i m e h c e l c i t u c
```

candle	cathedral	animal
cripple	cubicle	chemical
dismal	drizzle	cuticle
example	final	**eagle**
jewel	jungle	gentle
mammal	nostril	logical
riddle	rival	physical
several	signal	several
struggle	tunnel	speckle
		utensil

Connect the correct "uhl" sound ending

samp		canc
penc	il	Bib
rif	al	tunn
fin	el	kett
wrest	le	decim
music		sprink
pood	il	practic
utens	al	puzz
litt	el	mamm
cutic	le	vow
chemic		sign
nostr		sever
tons		anim

Answers in the back of the book.

Words ending in -ible or -able

able /ability

- after a **vowel ending** eg agreeable likeable

    agre**e** + able = agreeable
    lik**e** + able = likeable

- recently added words / **modern** words

    download + able = downloadable
    program + able = programmable

- 2 syllable words

- more common to add able

    variable   affordable   affordable
    removable   preventable   preventable
    reliable   reasonable   reasonable
                  enjoyable   enjoyable
    agre**ea**ble preferable   preferable
    lik**ea**ble probable   probability
                  suitable*   suitability
    networkable   capable*   capability
    downloadable fixable*   exceptions
    documentable
    computable
    microwavable
    programmable
    recyclable

ible / ibility

- when root word is not a complete word by itself
- 1 syllable words

    pos   possible   possibility
    ed   edible
    vis   visible   visibility
    cred   credible   credibility
    sponse   responsible   responsibility
    hor   horrible
    ter   terrible
    gul   gullible
    aud   audible
    flex   **flexible**   **flexibility**
    sense **sensible**   **sensibility**
    ***collect** ***collectible** Exceptions - root word is a complete word by itself.

    ~~fens~~   defensible   ⎫
    ~~vers~~   reversible   ⎬ If we strip these words
    ~~mis~~   permissible   ⎬ from their prefixes, the
    ~~vert~~   convertible   ⎬ root words are not
    ~~eleg~~   elegible   ⎬ complete words by
    ~~negli~~ negligible   ⎭ themselves.

Put the words in the right column

- program
- afford
- pos
- horror
- suit
- cape
- gul
- sense
- agree
- like
- rely
- vary
- document
- vision
- audio

able	ible

Answers in the back of the book.

Words ending in -ance -ancy or -ence -ency

-ance -ancy

- word ending with
  - **ation/ant**
  - **ear**
  - **a**
- If you are unsure, then you use this spelling. It is more common.

inst**ant**	instance	
radi**ant**	radiance	radiancy
signific**ant**	significance	significancy
toler**ant**	tolerance	
accept	acceptance	acceptancy
resembl	resemblance	etc.
insure	insurance	
enter	entrance	
perform	performance	
avoid	avoidance	
allow	allowance	
annoy	annoyance	
app**ear**	appearance	
hinder*	hinderance	
guide	guidance	
endure	endurance	

-ence -ency

- word ending with
  - **soft c and g (+ i, e or y)**
  - **ent**
  - **ere** or **er**

diff**er**	difference	
conf**er**	conference	
pref**er**	preference	preferency
ref**er**	reference	
exist	existence	existency
dili**ge**nt	diligence	diligency
intelli**ge**nt	intelligence	intelligency
inno**ce**nt	innocence	
compet**ent**	competence	competency
sil**ent**	silence	etc.
confid**ent**	confidence	
experim**ent**	experience	
abs**ent**	absence	
evid**ent**	evidence	
*correspond	correspondence	
*depend	dependence	dependency

Put the words in the right column

- instant
- insure
- competent
- absent
- guide
- endure
- significant
- exist
- differ
- evident
- refer
- avoid
- allow
- appear

ance	ence

you're amazing

Answers in the back of the book.

Crossword

Across

2. He got himself a good deal. He picked up that truck for a bar...

4. To live we all need water and ox......

5. The driver who will take you is also called the......

6. It appears in the sky with 7 beautiful colours.

8. We park the car in the g......

9. This winter we will go skiing and stay in our ..... (house in mountain)

11. In the day we wear clothes, but at night we wear p.....

14. He is my nephew and she is my n......

15. You pack your bags to go on holiday, in one hard cover container called a s....

17. He is going with a big ship around the world. He is going on a cr.....

19. There should be less war in this world. We should have more p.....

Down

1. Sometimes you can drink this water. Not always.

2. What is his faith? Christian, Jew, Muslim..... Another name for faith? be...

3. She only eats a long bread with cheese for lunch called a ba.....

5. They drink this bubbly wine when celebrating.

7. She makes many different designs with lots of different colours. She is cre....

10. Can I have another slice of cake p......?

12. When the boat stopped, the fisherman threw in the a......

13. When you pay for lunch, you need to ask for the payslip called a re.......

16. Another name for tummy starting with st....

18. You have to eat all of your vegetables, including these round green things. p....

Answers in the back of the book.

Numbers Days Months Seasons Abbreviations

first	Monday	Jan**u**ary	Mr.	Mister
second	Tuesday	Febr**u**ary	Mrs.	Missus
third	Wednesday	March	Ms.	Miss
fourth	Thursday	April	ASAP	As soon as possible
fifth	Friday	May	n/a	not available or not applicable
twentieth	Saturday	June		
sixtieth	Sunday	July	DIY	Do It Yourself
		August	Dr.	Doctor
Spring		September		
Summer		October		
Autumn		November		
Winter		De**ce**mber		

Friday, at the **end** of day, I see my

fri + end = **friends**

Mnemonics (Memory Strategies)

- ocean - **o**nly **c**rabs` **e**yes **a**re **n**arrow
- ne**cess**ary - prin**cess** has a **c**rown and **2 s**ocks

- c**e**m**e**t**e**ry - 3 e letters buried in cemetery
- **i**nquiry - **i**nvestigate
- **e**nquiry - request more information
- because - **b**ig **e**lephants **c**an **a**lways **u**nderstand **s**mall **e**lephants
- t**h**ere - **h**ere
- they`re - they are
- their - the**i**r = people
- be**lie**ve - never believe a **lie**

- laugh - **l**ots of **a**nts **u**nder **G**arrith`s **h**at

- rhythm - **r**hythm **h**elps **y**our **t**wo **h**ips **m**ove
- people - **p**ink **e**lves **o**nly **p**lay **l**ate **e**vening
- again - A **gain** like in climbing. a moun**tain** again.
- friend - **fri**/days are for friends at the **end** of the week
- difficulty - Mr. **D**, Mr. **I**, Mr. **FFI**, Mr. **C**, Mr. **U**, Mr. **LTY**
- ough - **O**h **U** **g**rumpy **h**amster!

With these words, you can learn a new word every two weeks. Just add it to your spelling list.

The challenge is on!!

busy
business
busier

beautiful
difficult
young
touch
neighbour
jealousy
impossible
nonsense (no sense)
because
friend
unfortunately
cousin
niece is nice
aunt
useful
once (one)
extremely
acceptable
excited
excess
suggest

beige

answer
sword
sugar
sandwich

anyone
anybody
anything

everyone
everybody
everything
everywhere

someone
somebody
something
somewhere

calendar (dates)
separate (rat)
interest
address (add)
perculiar (liar)
opposite ("i" sits opposite "e")
pressure (press)
ear hear heard
disappear
favourite (flavour)
island (land surrounded by sea)
accident (dent in car)
different (rent)

Can`t hear these sounds
arabesque
antique
cheque
tongue
rogue
league
boutique
meringue

Abide by the rules
courageous

Rule breakers
acknowledgment (no e)
judgment (no e)
goes

Always put words in context by phrasing a sentence. Use the same sentence every time you refer to that word.

homophones
scent and sent
seen and scene
weather and whether
who`s and whose
effect and affect
medal and meddle
accept and except
he`ll heal and heel
great and grate
knot and not
hear and here
groan and grown
mane and main
mist and missed
brake and break
male and mail
guessed and guest
jeans and genes
patients and patience
allowed and aloud
desert and dessert
herd and heard
advice and advise
compliment and complement

Investigate the difference between these words.
loose and lose
lightning and lightening
breath and breathe
mussel and muscle
angel and angle

ise or ize?
Some verbs can be spelt with either, but some verbs only ise. So use "ise" if you are not sure. The US use ize as the standard spelling.
revise
disguise
advise
finalise/finalize
equalize/equalise

hyphen or not?
Some words can be written both ways.
email/e-mail
co-operate/cooperate
pre-arranged/prearranged

"e" and "or" sound - with different spellings

treasure
pleasure
leisure
wear
swear
pear
tear
bear
heaven
heavy
death
dead
wealth
health
instead
spread
weather
leather

head
bread
meadow

breast
sweat

ready
steady
cleanse

BUT
heart

beware
care
dare
spare
scare
stare
square

pair
chair
fairy
stairs
air
fair
dairy
hair
repaired

snore
store

floor
door

pour

These words should be covered last in all of the curriculum of first words. They are often responsible for making learning to spell a difficult task. It can create a lot of confusion. By the time you have finished this spelling book, the photographic memory is more developed, books have been read containing these words, and it is no longer an "effort" for the brain to remember that these words are written like this. They may look like they don`t fit in any particular pattern we have learned so far but we can now recall them from memory with ease.

The most important aspect of spelling is building confidence. Every time a word is written correctly, confidence is built!

From here onwards...looking at morphemes to build your vocabulary. We should never stop learning!

Answers

frown	spouse
hour	brown
cloud	flower
town	round
mouse	power
sour	trout
down	mouth
clown	vowel
drown	flour
our	tower

Answers for ow o_e oa & oe

toe	note	globe	rainbow
tomatoes	heroes	yellow	bone
burrow	drone	pillow	tow
shadow	oak	oats	throw
envelope	elbow	arrow	
boat		loaf	

Answers

- narrow
- borrow
- borough
- burrow
- hope
- slowly
- toad
- shallow
- grown
- Follow
- home

The brown owl flew through the cloud down to the ground.

He saw a big, brown, fat mouse. He shouted at the mouse. Then he flew with all his power up to the tower.

The man came out of the house and frowned at the cow.

Everyone looked down to the ground with a frown making no sound.

I hope to follow the rainbow. My shadow, slowly follows me.

Answers - ough aught ought

- bought
- brought
- tough
- though
- thought
- taught
- through
- dough
- ploughs
- enough
- enough
- rough
- rough

Answers

1. The blue statue was captured in a picture. (4)
2. We panic every time she drives down the avenue to the venue. (3)
3. It is always an adventure tracking down crawling creatures. (2)
4. The energetic boy likes riding his bicycle. (1)
5. I know a trick that he already knew. (3)
6. I throw the ball to him. He can catch a few balls. (2)
7. I like eating green peas. (1)
8. The world will be a better place if there is more peace. (1)
9. I always give my friend a bigger piece of cake. (1)
10. He is very polite. He always says please. (1)

Answers

- believe
- belief
- conceive
- ceiling
- piece
- niece
- perceive
- deceit
- receipt
- shield
- grief
- yield
- received

ie	ei
believe	conceive
belief	ceiling
piece	perceive
niece	deceit
shield	receipt
grief	received
yield	

Answers

il ir im in anti dis un mis de

disappear
incapable
irresponsible
impossible
indecisive
misbehave
misunderstand
defrost
unequal
incorrect

illegal
irregular
impolite
antisocial
immature
inedible
disrespect
insane
illogical
inactive

Answers

The brochure of the chalet in the mountains looked beautiful. The chauffeur gave me a glass of champagne on our drive to the chalet.

The chef prepared a meal while we were busy parachute jumping.

I hope that we can fit it all into our schedule.

He was very positive about the expensive detective work that was done.

They used the latest technology mixed with chemistry and got great results.

The school choir and the orchestra perform at the same time.

The brain can be trained to be more positive.

You are the captain of your ship.

Refrain from drinking from the fountain - the water is not clean.

Crossword Answers

Answers

tion
combination
devotion
correction
education

cian
electrician
politician
mathematician
beautician

electric
combine
revise
explode
suspense
politics
devote
correct
mathematic
educate
decide
supervise
beauty

sion
revision
explosion
decision
supervision

cion
suspicion

Answers

tial	cial
torrential	special
circumstantial	
initial	especially
	social
partial	
	official
confidential	

Answers

sample	cancel
pencil	Bible
rifle	tunnel
final	kettle
wrestle	decimal
musical	sprinkle
poodle	practical
utensil	puzzle
little	mammal
cuticle	vowel
chemical	signal
nostril	several
tonsil	animal

Answers

able	ible
programmable	possible
affordable	horrible
suitable	gullible
capable	sensible
agreeable	visible
likeable	audible
reliable	
variable	
documentable	

Answers

ance	ence
instance	competence
insurance	absence
guidance	existence
endurance	difference
significance	evidence
avoidance	reference
allowance	
appearance	

you're amazing

Crossword Answers

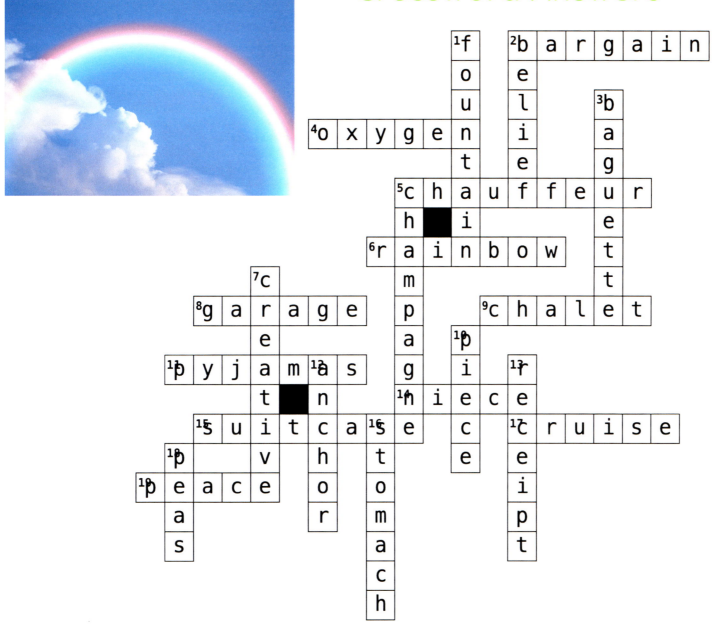

A Logical Approach to Spelling

You can contact us by email.
info@logicalapproachtolearning.com
2024 Jurina Dean
You can follow us on Instagram logicalapproachtospelling